MARC HAGAN-GUIREY

# LE CORBUSIER PAPER MODELS

## 10 KIRIGAMI BUILDINGS TO CUT AND FOLD

LAURENCE KING PUBLISHING

# HOW TO USE THIS BOOK

One of the essential factors in successfully cutting kirigami is preparation. Setting up the right environment and ensuring that you have everything you need within reach will help you focus on your work. Make sure that you're working in a suitably well-lit room. You might be surprised to find that that even thin paper can cast a shadow long enough to hinder your scoring when working on small scales. Try to wear short sleeves and lose any bracelets that might snag on paper elements. You might want to put on some music when you're working – I love listening to film soundtracks.

Most importantly, take your time and have lots of breaks. Cutting on such a small scale can be quite intense, so when you feel a little tired or frustrated just go and pop the kettle on.

If you accidentally cut something incorrectly, don't despair. Finish the model off and use some sticky tape to put it back together. If you use the method below, you can preserve the templates in the book and give it another go if you make a big mistake.

*Villa Savoye, 1931 (see p.11)*

## Paper

The weight of the paper (or g/m²) is incredibly important when making kirigami. Not any old sheet of printer paper will do. It needs to be sturdy enough to support itself but also not so thick that it's too difficult to cut through. The templates in this book are printed on 200 g/m² paper, so if you want to keep the book intact by not removing the templates then I suggest scanning or photocopying the model and reprinting it on a paper stock somewhere between 180 and 220 g/m².

## Tools

**X-Acto knife and blades** – Buy in bulk and save yourself the drama of realizing that you've run out of fresh blades just as you've broken the last one – tips can snap off with just a little too much pressure. Always use a sharp one because it makes cutting so much easier. Blunt blades never cut paper as crisply.

**Self-healing cutting mat** – I really advise getting one of these. I once got hot glue on the dining table and my mum went ballistic. You can get an A4-sized mat for around £3. It'll protect the work surface and will also prolong the life of your blades.

**Metal ruler** – Get a good-quality metal ruler because blades can easily slip off course and take a chunk out of plastic ones. Plastic ones rarely have a true straight edge, either. One piece of advice is to keep the ruler clean. Metal rulers pick up bits of grime that can end up transferring to your nice clean paper.

**Skewers** – Food skewers or toothpicks are really useful for popping out small creases or keeping folds from wrongly inverting as you fold opposing planes.

**Bone folder** – This isn't essential but helps to create nice crisp folds without using mucky fingers.

## Terminology

You should familiarize yourself with these terms, as I'll be using them in the folding instructions.

The **template** is printed on the reverse of the model. When you display it, you'll be looking at the blank side of the paper.

The **horizon** is the main 90° fold that forms the flat base that the model sits on and the vertical upright part of the model. In simpler terms, it's the fold between the 'sky' and the 'land' of the finished model. The horizon folds are the outermost folds, and usually the starting point for folding.

The **background plane** is the 'sky' and the vertical, standing section of the model.

The **base plane** is the 'floor' or 'ground' on which the model stands.

**Facades** are the vertical 'walls' of the model. They're usually forward-facing and might feature doors or windows.

**Roof planes** are essentially the horizontal parts on top of the model.

**Structural lines** are those lines printed in black, and are the ones that you cut through completely.

## Cutting and scoring

It's usually best to start cutting the structural lines at the centre of the model and working outwards.

### Half-cutting

Half-cutting is when you score a line that cuts only halfway through the paper. This makes it easy for the paper to fold, making a hinge at 90°. Before starting a project, experiment with half-cutting on some paper of a similar weight to the models. You'll eventually master how much pressure to apply without cutting all the way through. It's important to remember that even if you're familiar with a certain type of paper, the sharpness of the blade you're using will produce different results. You may want to reserve a blunt blade for this task.

### Mountain folds and valley folds

Valley folds (blue dashed lines) are half-cut on the printed side of the template. The fold is pushed inwards like a valley. Mountain folds (red dotted lines) are half-cut on the non-printed side and pushed outwards like a mountain peak.

### Marking mountain scores

Because the template is only printed on one side, you'll need to make some small incisions on the back of the card to mark out where you need to perform half-cutting for mountain folds on the non-printed side. On the printed side of the template, use the tip of the blade to make a small incision at both ends of the mountain fold (red dotted line). Flip the paper to see the two small holes. Line up your ruler between these two points and perform the half-cut. For long mountain folds, I suggest creating an additional two or three markers along the length of the line.

### Folding

The most important thing to remember is that you should never crease the folds sharply in the first instance. Start by applying a little pressure and help them move in the direction you want. Gently work your way around the various folds of the model, returning to the beginning and applying a little more pressure to the crease each time. You might do this two or three times before the model is complete. I refer to this as progressive folding.

## Folding techniques

Much of the time, the best method for folding a crease will feel very intuitive. Below, I've created a few names for techniques that I'll refer to in the folding instructions.

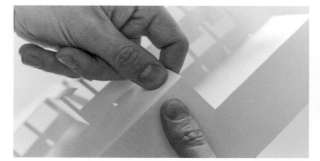

*Lever* – Using a forefinger behind the fold as a lever, push down the background plane with your forefinger and the base plane with the thumb of your other hand.

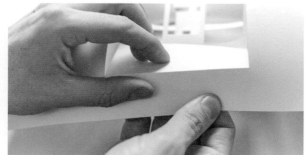

*Push out* – Holding the model in one hand, use the fingers of the other to push one side of the paper along the fold. You'll have to gradually work along the fold in some cases. This technique is mainly used for valley folds.

*Pinch* – Although I'll rarely recommend pinching the crease, sometimes this technique is perfectly acceptable to use on smaller mountain or valley folds.

*Springing* – Push two planes of paper that are on the same axis together by holding each plane in both hands and moving them towards each other. Then allow the paper to spring back to its original position. Like progressive folding, you'll need to do this a few times before it keeps its shape.

*Skewer* – This technique is essentially the same as the lever, but where the space is too small to fit your finger in you can use a skewer or toothpick to pop elements out.

# MAISON CITROHAN

Concept model, 1920

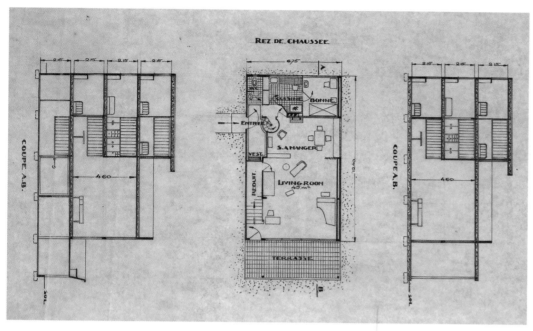

Floor plans

In 1920, Le Corbusier and his cousin Pierre Jeanneret exhibited their concept for Maison Citrohan in an effort to improve living standards after World War I. It was an exercise in efficient living spaces, and the name was inspired in part by Citroën cars, which Le Corbusier regarded as exemplary in efficiency. Much like a car, this social-housing prototype was designed in such a way that it could also be mass-produced in a factory. The result of the concept would be a product that was more affordable to the working class.

While his work was in constant evolution, there's a clear distinction in Le Corbusier's ideology after 1915. At this point, several influential projects steered him more closely towards the radical thinking that would define the rest of his career.

The architect's earlier Dom-ino system, a portmanteau of the Latin word *domus* and innovation, was one such project that became instrumental in his approach to construction. The moniker also evoked dominoes, which can be stacked during a game to create a free-standing structure. At its core, the Dom-ino was essentially a skeleton frame that required no internal load-bearing walls – instead, vertical columns would bear the weight of reinforced-concrete slabs creating the floors. This ingenious system would free up the interior space to be used as effectively as possible. Citrohan is a manifestation of this system.

The Citrohan went through several revisions. This kirigami model is based on the 1922 iteration, in which the body of the house is raised on pillars, therefore creating a ground-level floor with functional spaces such as garage and pantry.

The first floor proposes a small kitchen and bathroom, while the main living space is accentuated by a double-height ceiling. An enclosed staircase (earlier versions had the stair on the exterior) extends from the ground floor to the top. A master suite and lounge area occupy the second floor, and on top sit the 'children's' bedrooms. The third floor also enjoys a roof terrace.

Citrohan model

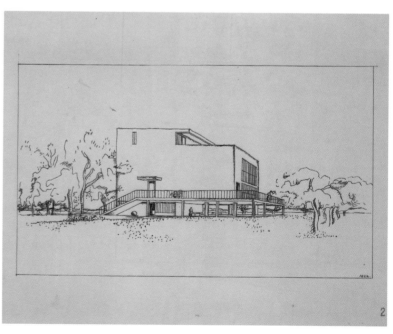

Citrohan sketch

# MAISON CITROHAN

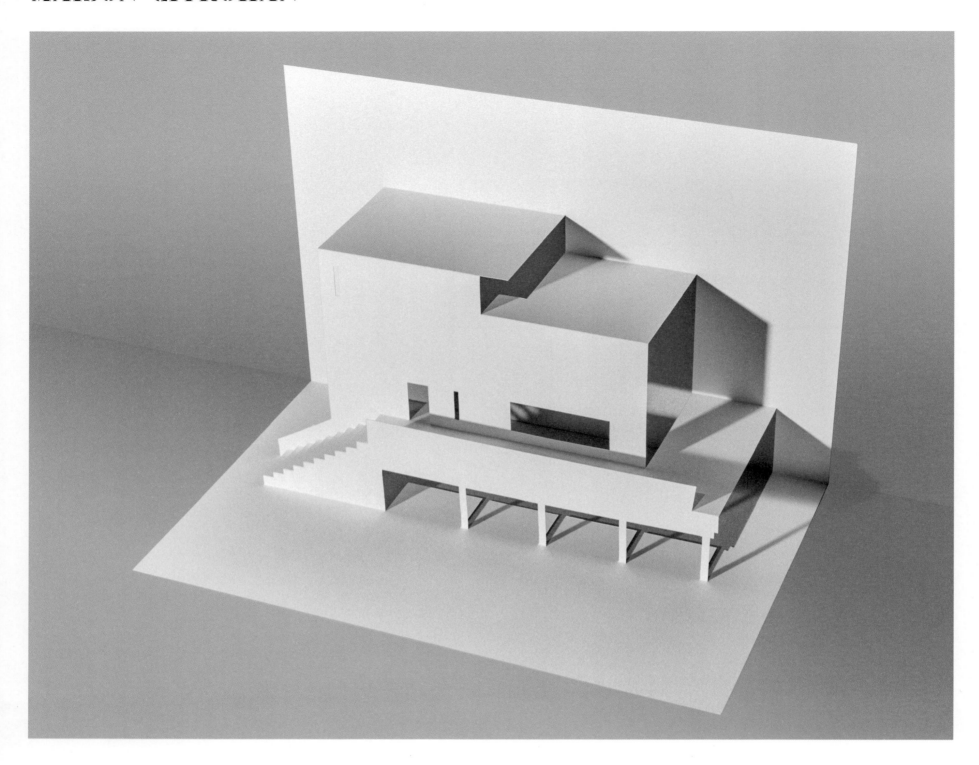

## Folding guide

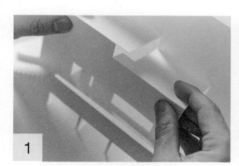

**1**

With the printed side facing you, lever fold the horizon valley folds then turn the template over to the blank side and lever fold the mountain folds on the top of the building.

**2**

Lever fold the mountain fold on the balcony on the right, then work your way across to the left side.

**3**

Form the staircase by pushing together the two planes in a springing action.

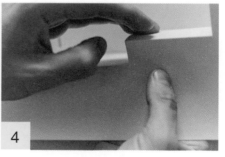

**4**

Flip the template over and push out the valley folds at the top and bottom of the building.

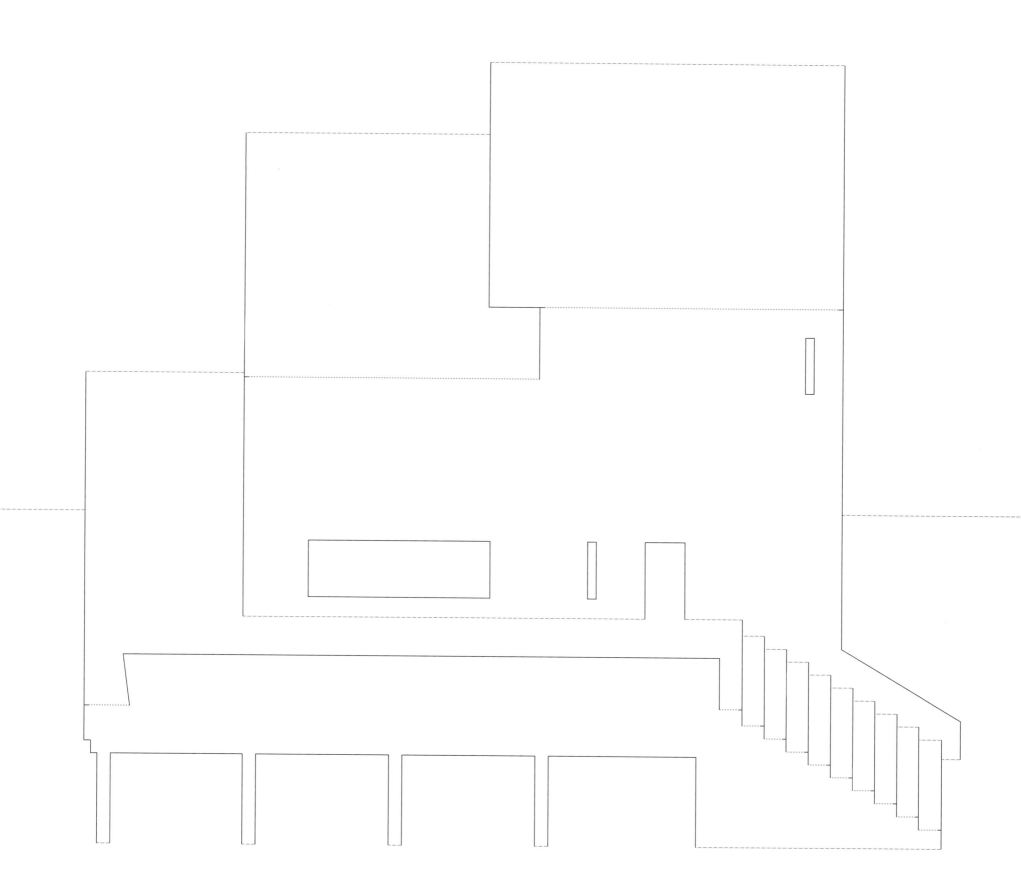

# VILLA STEIN-DE MONZIE

Garches, France, 1927

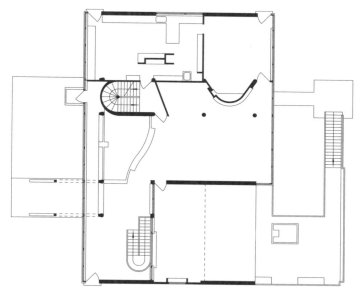

Ground-floor plan

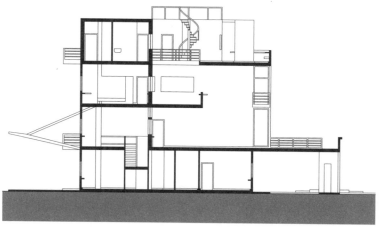

Section

In 1918, Le Corbusier and painter Amédée Ozenfant pioneered the art form Purism in their book *Après le Cubisme* (After Cubism). By the 1920s, Le Corbusier's notoriety had spread far and wide – and the patronage of wealthy clients in pursuit of cutting-edge design allowed him to explore Purism in his architecture.

Gabrielle de Monzie, Michael Stein and his wife, Sarah, often took joint holidays, and in 1927 they approached Le Corbusier and Pierre Jeanneret to design them a holiday retreat in Garches, Paris.

Villa Stein-de Monzie, also known as Garches, mostly comprises a large white cube. As with Le Corbusier's other Purist villas, it was designed using the Dom-ino system of Maison Citrohan, with a series of pillars supporting concrete-slab floors and allowing the facades to be non-structural. This is evident in the uninterrupted ribbon windows running the full length of the house, which would be impossible with load-bearing outer walls.

On the ground level is a garage and two entrances set almost symmetrically in the facade. While the smaller door is for servants, guests are greeted by a long cantilevered porch leading into an oversized entry hall. Unusual angled and curved walls bounce the visitor towards the large curving staircase leading up to the reception rooms and kitchen. At the rear of the building, a staircase leads to the sheltered terrace – and provided the inspiration for this kirigami.

The roof terraces are divided by linear and curved walls (the curved-ended shape houses a sauna). These geometrical shapes are an obvious reference to the design of the ocean liners that Le Corbusier championed in his self-published periodical *L'Esprit Nouveau* (The New Spirit). It's also notable that the machine-inspired aesthetic of the terrace resembles his Purist paintings – flat and smooth curves stripped of unnecessary ornamentation. Academics comment that Garches can be viewed like a three-dimensional Purist painting: the skyline forms a backdrop, and the building is a composition of layered facades. In many ways, this is exactly how a kirigami model is designed.

Steps leading to rear terrace

Interior ribbon windows

# VILLA STEIN-DE MONZIE

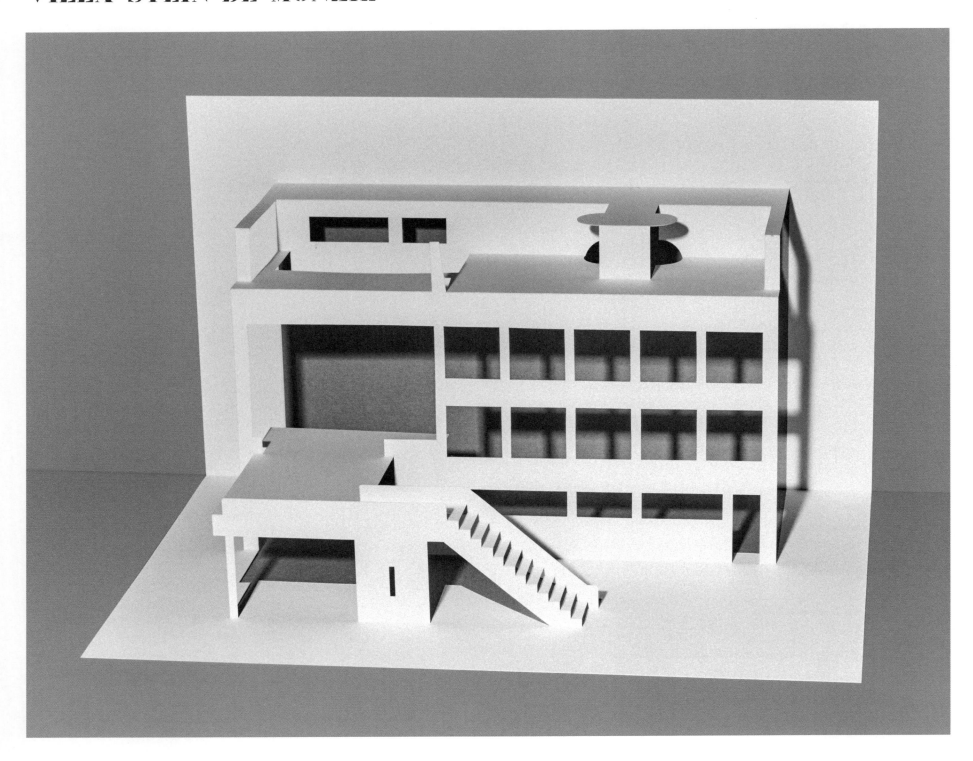

## Folding guide

**1** With the printed side facing you, lever fold the two horizon valley folds then push out all the valley folds at the base of the building – include the pillars and the bottom of the staircase.

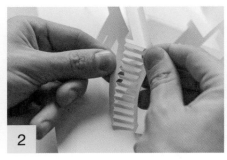

**2** Start forming the staircase by alternating between the front and back, gradually teasing it into shape while also spring folding the planes together.

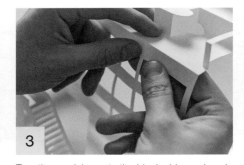

**3** Turn the model over to the blank side, and work your way across the top mountain fold that forms the edge of the rooflines.

**4** Work down from the top of the model to the base, alternating between the various mountain and valley folds. It might help to spring together the upper portion of the building to guide it into shape.

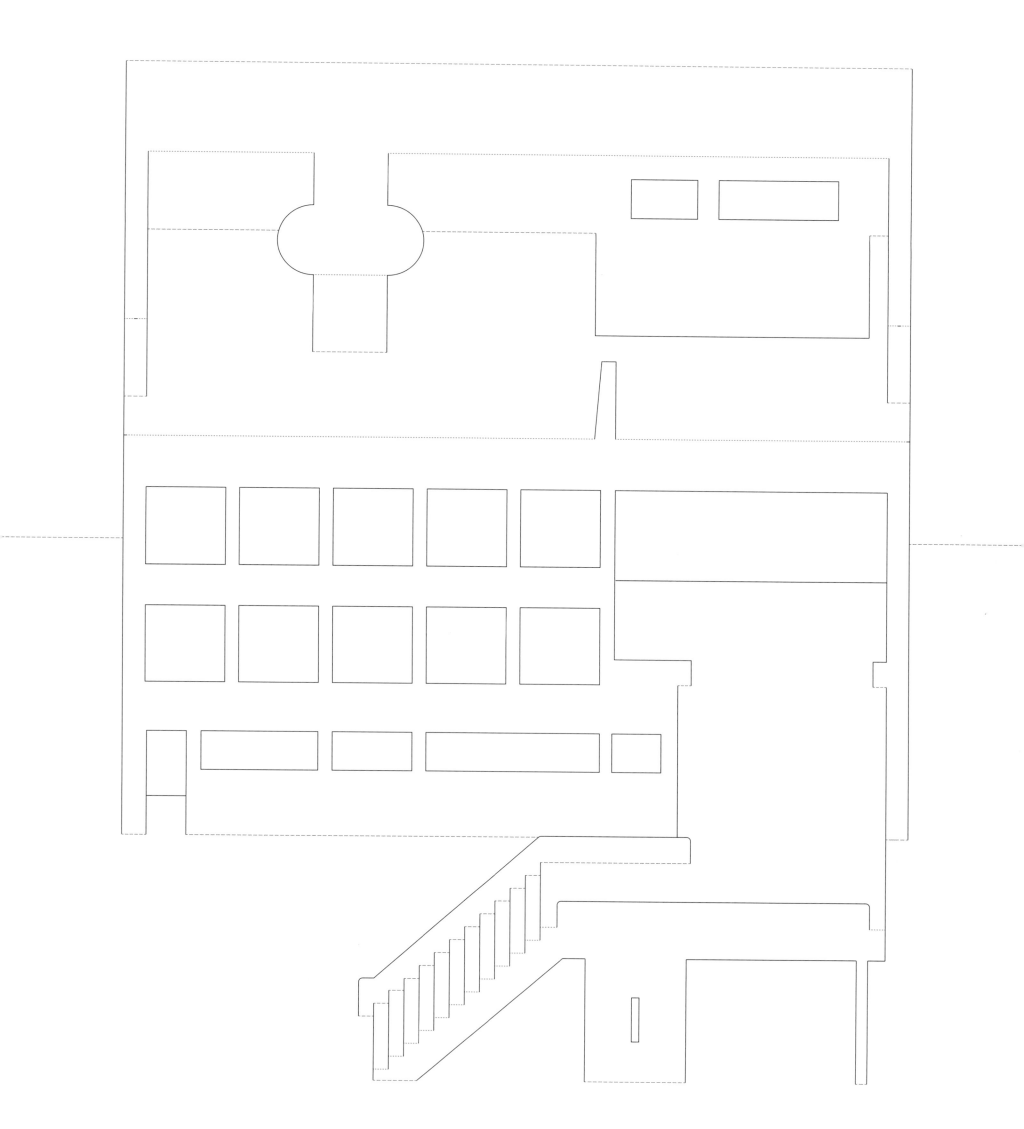

# VILLA SAVOYE

Poissy, France, 1931

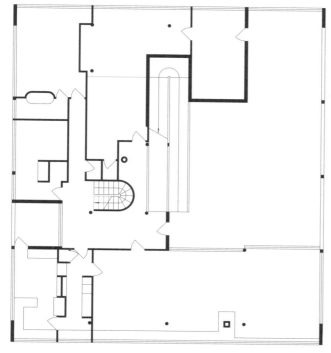

First-floor plan

South-east elevation

Villa Savoye is not only Le Corbusier's and Pierre Jeanneret's best-known house, but also one that would define the course of modern architecture. Built two years after Villa Stein-de Monzie, Savoye would be the last of the Purist white villas and what Le Corbusier saw as the ultimate in modern living.

The wealthy Savoye family commissioned a weekend retreat in Poissy, a small suburb north-west of Paris. Their brief stipulated no more than 'sufficient space for servants' quarters'. While they were said to have had no preconceptions about the outcome, they were obviously drawn towards the architect's much-lauded concept of 'a machine for living in'. Spiralling costs meant that the project reached a staggering 900,000 francs, but its owners received one of the most iconic buildings in modern history.

In 1923 Le Corbusier produced his modern-architecture manifesto, *Vers une Architecture* (Towards a New Architecture). In it, he outlines his Five Points of architecture for a truly modern-day building: 1) the house's mass lifted up on pilotis, thin reinforced-concrete stilts that freed up space beneath; 2) a free floor plan, meaning no load-bearing walls; 3) a roof garden affording views of the surrounding area; 4) ribbon windows horizontally wrapping the building, providing views, light and ventilation; and 5) a free facade, meaning that structural support was provided by concrete pillars and not the exterior walls.

Villa Savoye embodies all these aspects. Its smooth white cuboid structure with ship-like 'funnels' sits on thin concrete struts. The exterior's crisp edges bear no mouldings or ornamentation. Set behind the columns, a horseshoe-shaped ground floor allows a car to sweep past the curved main entrance and, after the passengers disembark, continue around to the large garage.

The most prominent interior feature is that the house contains both a staircase and a ramp. This slow-climbing ramp provides gradual movement through the building. The architect describes it as an architectural promenade: a journey through the house punctuated by moments where light penetrates in a different way.

Side elevation

Living area, looking onto the roof terrace

# VILLA SAVOYE

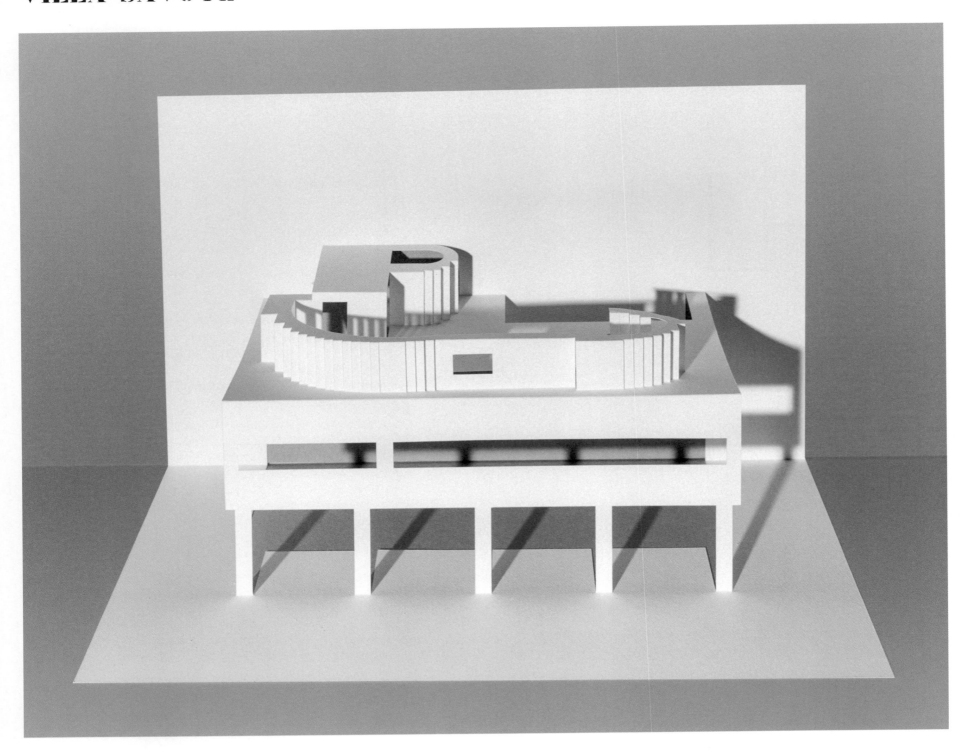

## Folding guide

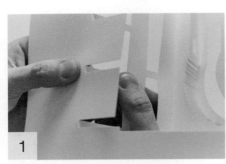

**1**

With the printed side facing you, start by lever folding the two horizon valley folds followed by the valley folds that form the pillars of the building.

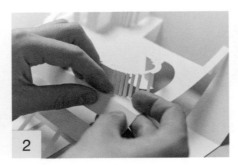

**2**

Flip the model over and fold the mountain fold that runs along the front edge of the building. Turn the template over and push out all the valley folds that connect the building to the background plane.

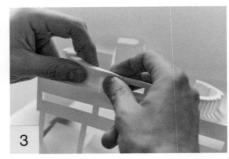

**3**

Spring fold together the section that looks like a letter 'P' from above.

**4**

Gradually work your way around the large sweeping curve, pinching together the small mountain folds.

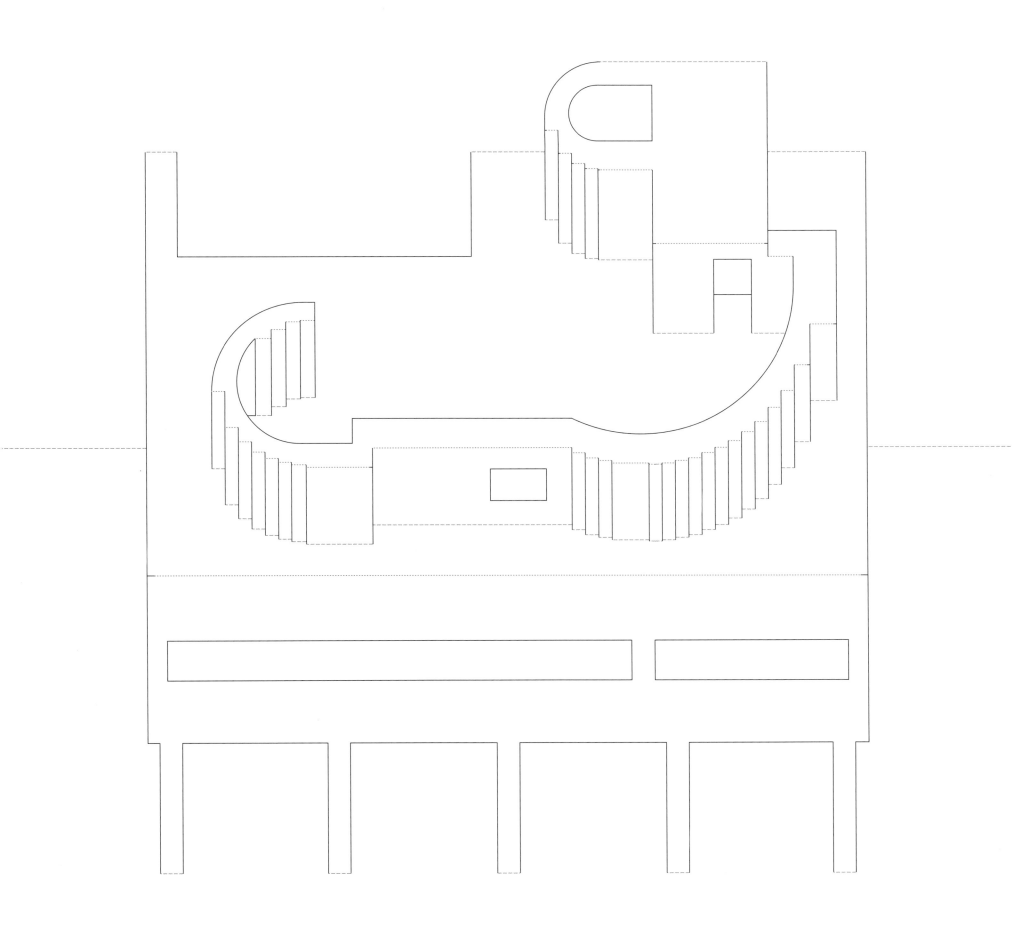

# MAISON DE WEEK-END

La Celle-Saint-Cloud, France, 1934

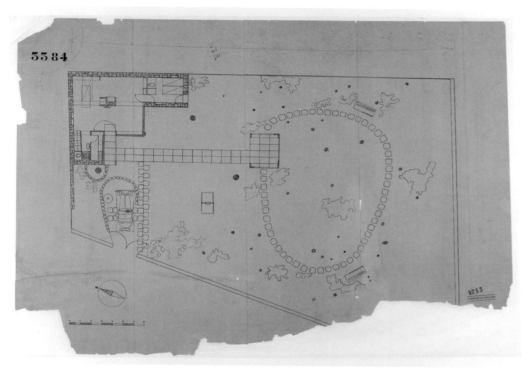

Building and garden plan

This diminutive but influential house was commissioned by M. Félix, a director of the bank Société Henfel, and was designed as a weekend getaway from the bustle of the capital's centre. At only 2.4 metres (8 feet) high, the rear corner of the house reaches level with the high perimeter wall and is sheltered by the trees of its garden.

Because of the use of quarry stone, masonry and a turf-covered roof, the residence could easily be mistaken for a cave dwelling or hermit's hut. This aesthetic was not an accident, and the intention was to contrast with the surrounding bourgeois villas. Despite its rustic appearance and materials, Maison de Week-end is an extremely sophisticated project in both its engineering and its construction methods – a mixture of industrial technology with pre-industrial building techniques. Its success would mean that Le Corbusier would reinvent its style and method in projects such as Villa Sarabhai and Maisons Jaoul roughly two decades later.

As Maison de Week-end appears to be built into the landscape, the true form of the house is something of a mystery, though a visitor can deduce that it is almost L-shaped in arrangement. The inside of the 'L' faces the garden and the rear is integrated into the corner of the boundary walls. A skylight brings light into the deepest part of the house. In contrast to the quarry stone, another wall of thick, mottled Nevada glass block allows more light to flood in.

The inside of the house is mostly a large square room flanked by two smaller extrusions leading off to the bedroom and service rooms of kitchen and bathroom. In contrast to the rugged exterior, the rooms are beautifully finished. A large brick central chimney stack divides the space. The house's most notable interior feature is its golden bent-plywood vaulted ceilings, which were inspired by Le Corbusier's trips to the Mediterranean.

Maison de Week-end is unfortunately no longer standing, having been demolished some time in the late twentieth century.

Interior showing the brick chimney stack

Isometric drawing

# MAISON DE WEEK-END

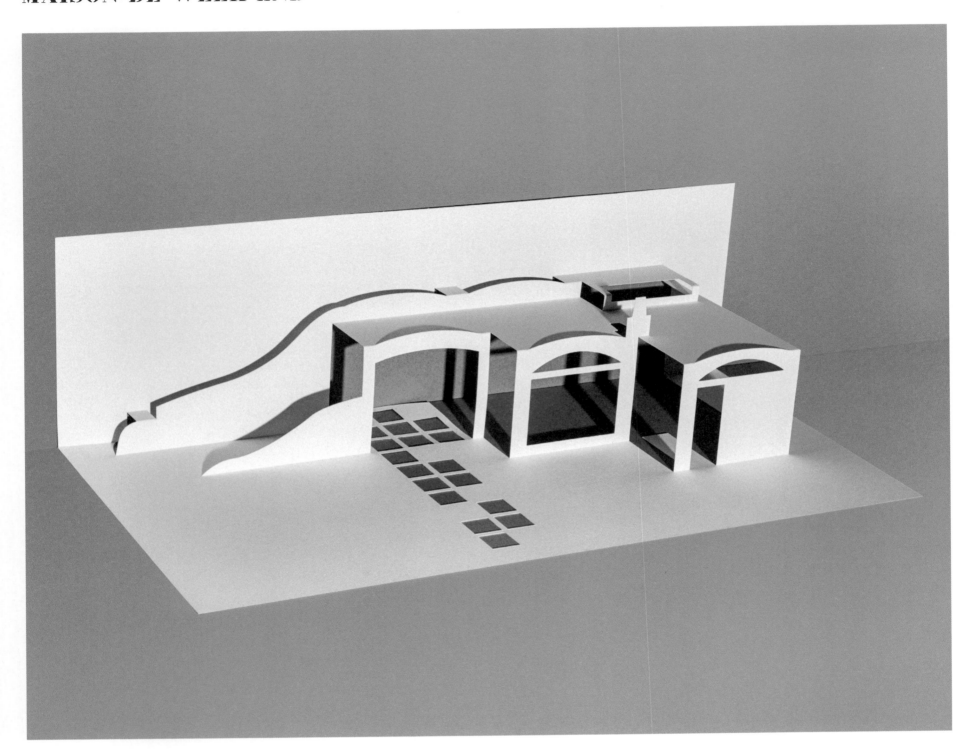

## Folding guide

1

With the printed side facing you, lever fold the two horizontal valley folds, followed by the valley fold at the base of the two sloping hill sections on the right.

2

Turn the model 180° and push out the valley folds that connect the back portion of the building to the background plane, as well as the valley folds at the base of the model.

3

Concentrate on the skylight section on the right of the model, first by pushing out the valley folds then by flipping the model over. It might help to use a skewer here, or to spring the planes together.

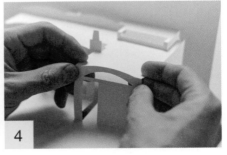

4

With the blank side of the model facing you, work along the mountain folds that form the top of the roof.

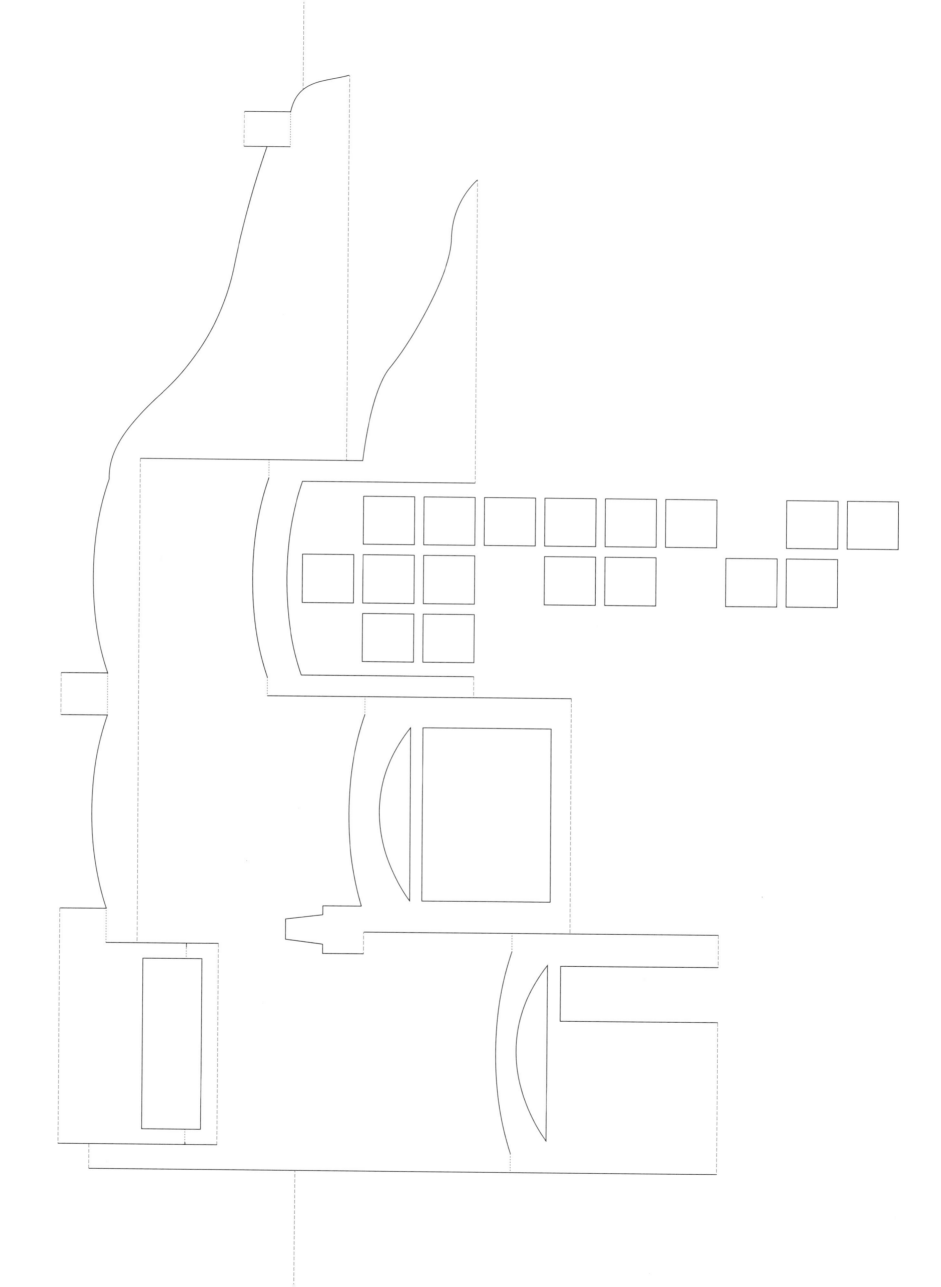

# MAISONS JAOUL

Neuilly-sur-Seine, France, 1951

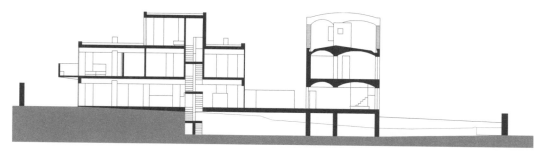

Section

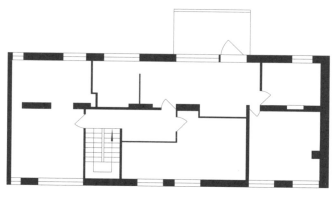

First-floor plan

Located in a desirable suburb just over 1.5 kilometres (1 mile) from Paris's Champs-Élysées, two houses – Las Casas A and B – sit on a small plot of 93 square metres (1,000 square feet). Based on Le Corbusier's Modulor system of human proportions, they were commissioned by André Jaoul for his and his son Michel's families.

From street level, a sloping walkway topped with several steps leads to a paved courtyard serving as the entrances to both units. Several metres apart, the two dwellings sit perpendicular to each other but are connected by a shared subterranean garage. Their overall appearance is highly sculptural; they are perforated with asymmetrical clusters of windows and wooden cladding of varying sizes. The three storeys are composed of raw brick and divided by a layer of thick concrete in the form of an elongated arc. Curiously, these layers give an X-ray clue to the buildings' interior forms. The two underside curves of these concrete slabs cut through from one end to the other, creating curved ceilings. Internally, these are permanently shuttered with bricks in the same style as the Catalan vaults that Le Corbusier had discovered during an excursion to Spain. The units' various rooftops are adorned with turf – recalling abandoned buildings being reclaimed by nature.

Maisons Jaoul are significant in Le Corbusier's work because they mark an end to his white Purist villas of the 1920s, with their polished exteriors, and his transition to raw concrete, or *béton brut*. In post-war Europe, concrete and brick remained the cheapest and most accessible materials. This 'Brutalism' exposes the buildings' materials and construction to us, giving a skeletal effect, with nothing to hide.

For this reason, for the kirigami model I chose to represent La Casa A in a sectional cut format, stripping away its brick facade to expose the internal structural aspects. This way, you can see the central supporting spine and vaulted ceilings.

Maisons Jaoul was made a historical monument in 1966.

The exterior gives a clue to the interior form

Interior showing the Catalan vaulted ceilings

# MAISONS JAOUL

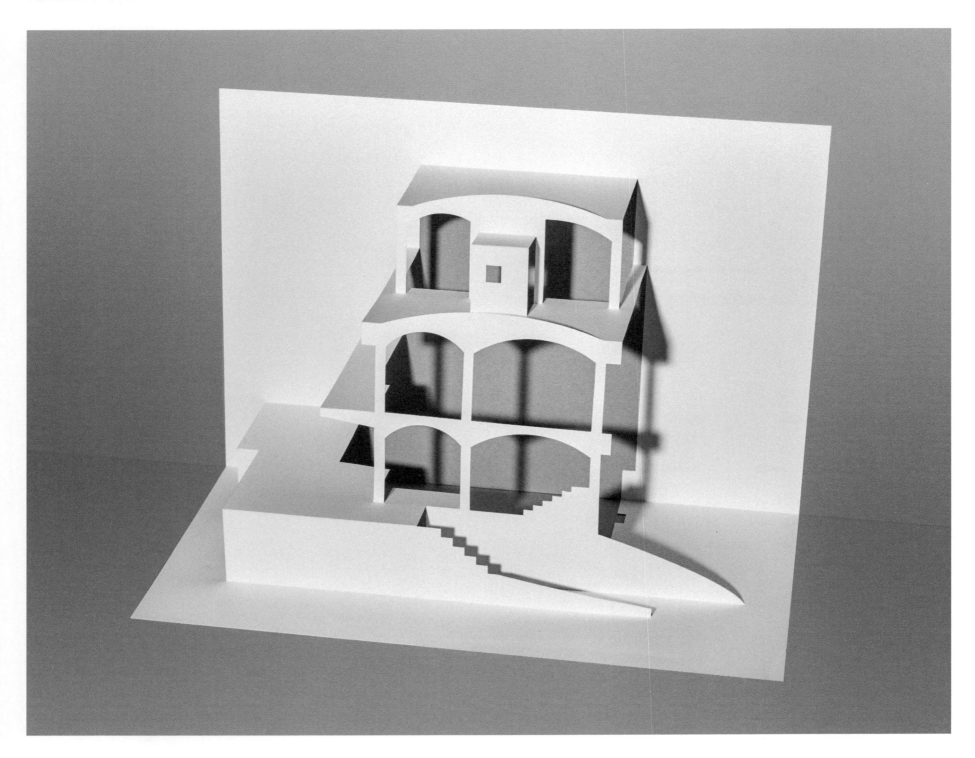

## Folding guide

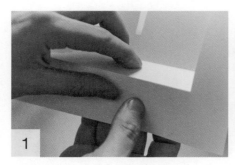

**1** With the printed side facing you, lever fold the horizon valley folds then push out the valley folds along the base of the building.

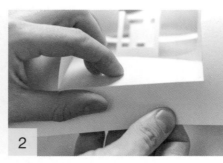

**2** Turn the template 180° and push out the valley fold that connects the top roof plane to the background plane.

**3** Lever fold the mountain folds along the roof edge on the blank side of the model, then work downwards through the others.

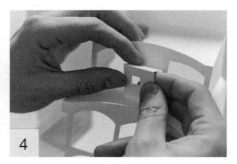

**4** Work the folds of the small cube near the top of the building, alternating between the front and the back of the template.

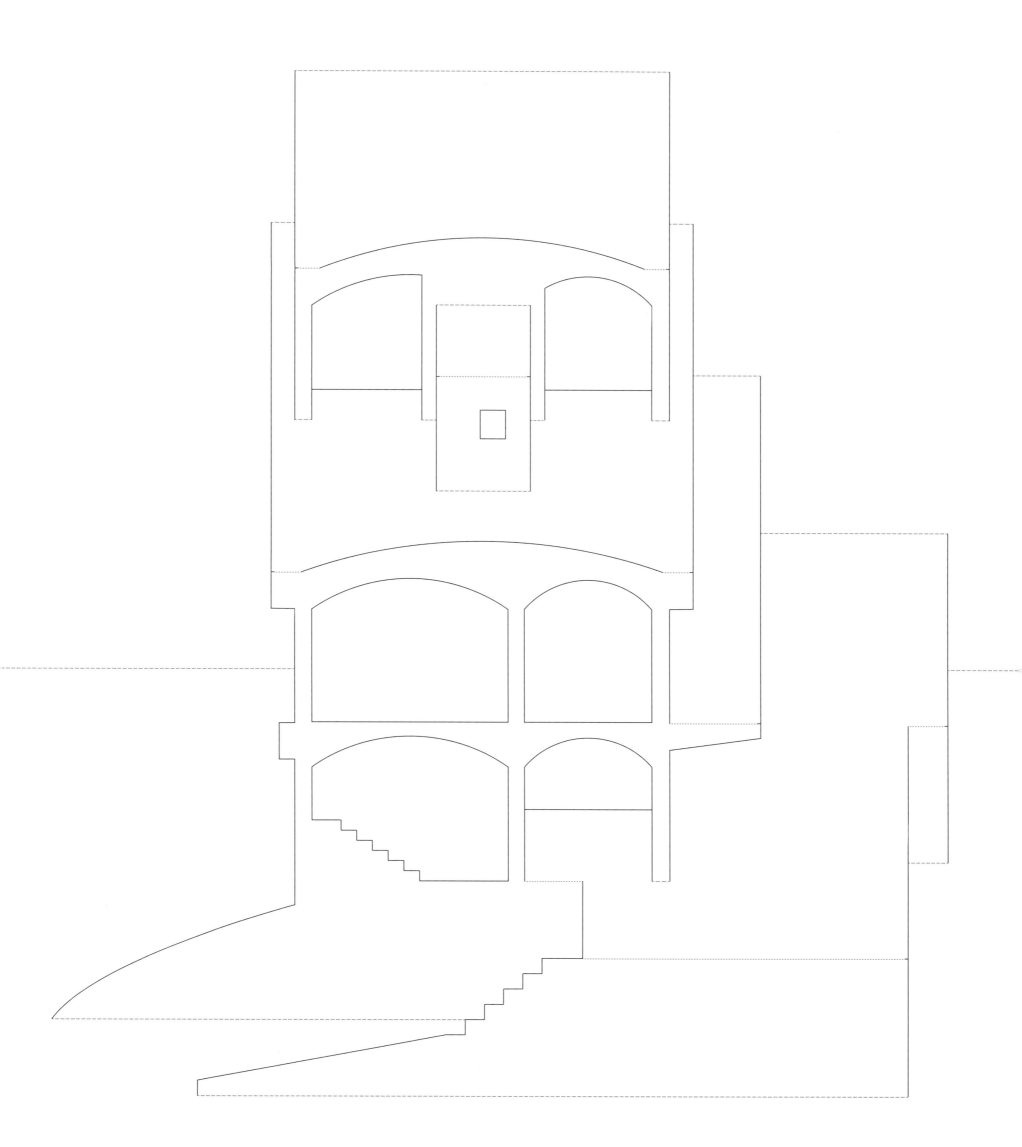

# UNITÉ D'HABITATION

Marseille, France, 1952

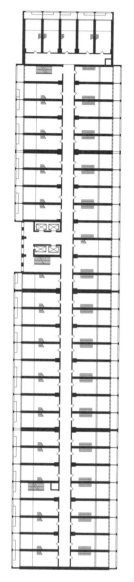

Typical floor plan for
the entire building

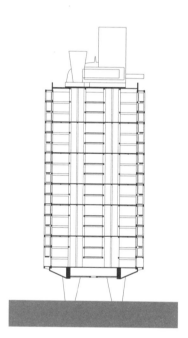

Section

Le Corbusier's commanding tower block in Marseille was the first of the Unités d'Habitation to be built. The building, also referred to as the Cité Radieuse (Radiant City), was his first large-scale high-density residential housing project to be commissioned by the French Government. The Marseille project is thought of as one of the most significant Brutalist buildings to be constructed, and on completion it became the 'poster child' for social housing around the world.

The Cité Radieuse epitomizes Le Corbusier's ideology of a 'machine for living in' on a grand scale. The building is an 18-storey linear block containing 337 apartments for around 1,600 residents. There are 23 varieties of apartments or *logements prolongés* (extended dwellings), ranging from single-occupant homes to those for families of ten. From the exterior, the grey of the concrete is punctuated by the colourful blocks of the balconies. This experimental building caters for both the community and the private needs of its residents. Designed as a 'vertical garden city', it contains 'streets' running the length of the building. On the 7th and 8th floors, there are commercial outlets such as a bakery, grocer, post office, hotel and doctor's surgery. As in the Purist villas that came before, the available space is maximized by populating the communal roof terrace with a gym, paddling pool and cafe – there's even a 300-metre (1,000-foot) running track. As at Villa Savoye and Villa Stein-de Monzie, Le Corbusier's admiration for steamships and industrial design is evident here in the mammoth funnel-like smoke stacks. The elements on the roof echo both ancient Greek temples and the modernity of industrial design.

The 'DNA' of Maison Citrohan is at the heart of the two-storey apartments. The double-height ceilings of the living rooms, with huge windows, give an enormous sense of space in otherwise narrow apartments. Most have two deep-set private balconies that allow air to flow from one side to the other.

The Unité d'Habitation was added to the UNESCO World Heritage list in 2016.

The communal roof terrace has
a gym, paddling pool and cafe

The building could be
mistaken for an ocean liner

# UNITÉ D'HABITATION

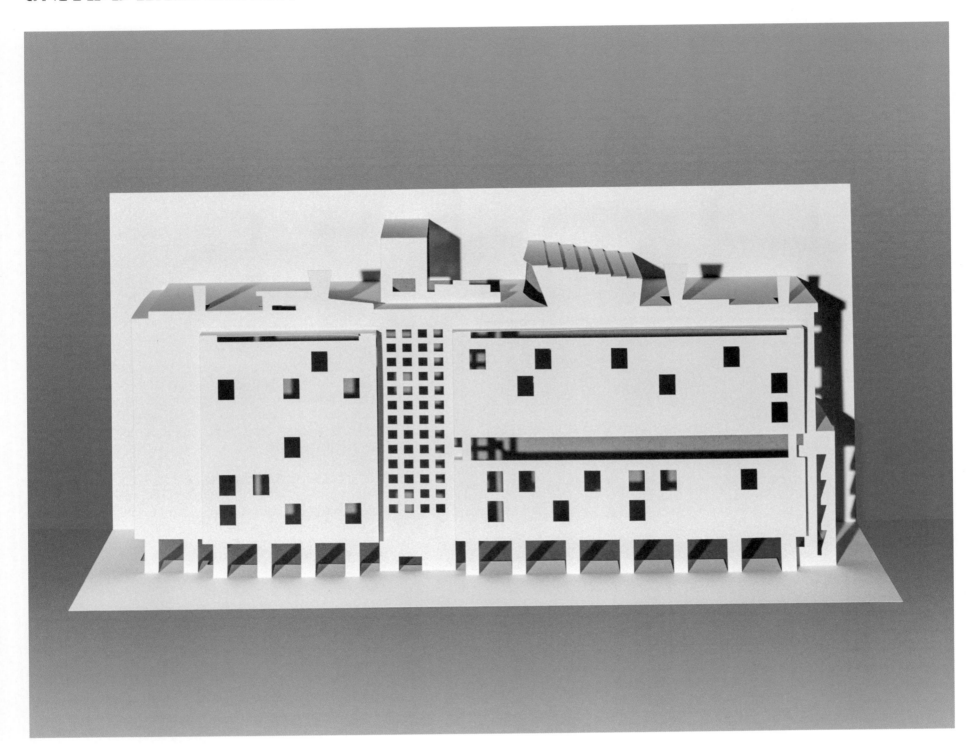

## Folding guide

1

With the printed side facing you, start by lever folding the two horizon valley folds and then work across the base of the building, pushing out the valley folds of the pillars along the base.

2

Turn the model over to the blank side and work along the top of the building, pinching together the mountain folds.

3

Still on the blank side, spring together the two small central folds that link the blocks together.

4

Pinch together the two protruding mountain folds at the front of the building.

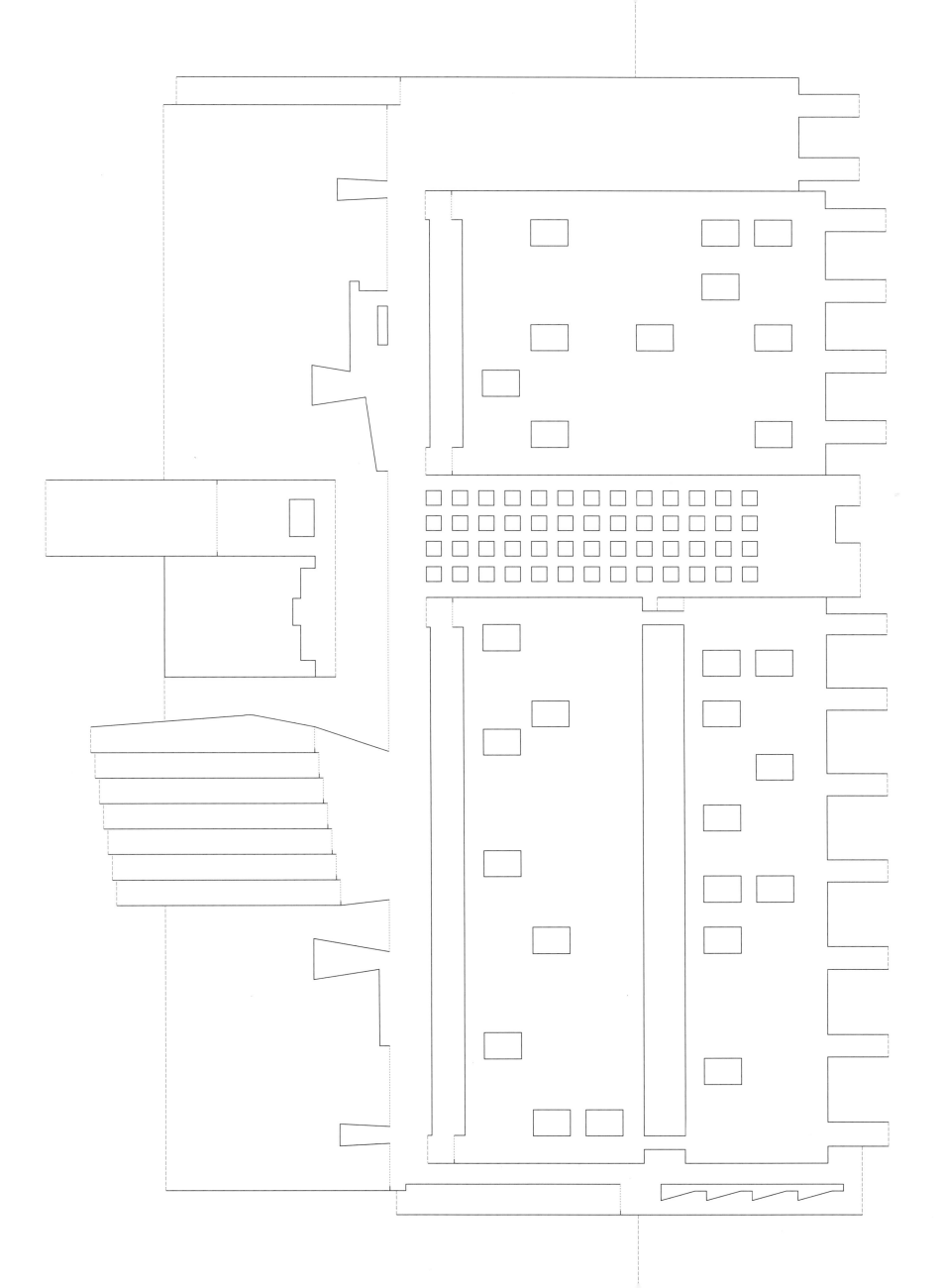

# MAISON DE LA CULTURE

Firminy, France, 1953

Drawing of the western facade
overhanging the steep hill

During World War II, Firminy, a mining town 9.6 kilometres (6 miles) from Saint-Étienne, suffered enormous damage. Eugène Claudius-Petit – a long-time supporter and friend of Le Corbusier and mayor of the town – recruited Le Corbusier to create a large complex as part of the new model town, which was to be known as Firminy-Vert. Incorporating a stadium, swimming pool, church and youth centre (or Maison de la Culture), the project would become Le Corbusier's largest urban architectural complex in Europe, and his second largest, after Chandigarh.

Maison de la Culture is striking in its appearance. Its 112-metre-long (370-foot) western and eastern facades are both canted, with the more extreme western side overhanging the edge of the steep hillside on which it is built. Observed from either gable end, a curved (or, rather, parabolic) concrete roof sweeps up towards the sky – a demonstration of remarkable engineering.

Along the two principal sides of the building are continuous series of tall vertical windows of varying widths – some clear, some filled with primary colours, yet all with mullions at varying heights. To the untrained eye these may appear random, but the truth is that they contain a hidden meaning. Calculated by Iannis Xenakis, a composer who had previously worked with Le Corbusier, the patterns in which they flow create a musical partition, thus ingeniously infusing music into the building.

A semi-abstract bas-relief on one gable end features natural elements typical of Le Corbusier's later painting style. A bull in the centre and angular branches with leaves stretch out to shapes such as faces, a human ear and a conch shell. You can see a simplified version of this in the kirigami model.

The building houses a music room, theatre, auditorium and bar. Inside, the canted west facade accommodates tiered seating. The youth centre was the only building in the complex to be completed in Le Corbusier's lifetime. Construction on the remainder was completed in 1969. Maison de la Culture was added to UNESCO's World Heritage list in 1984.

A semi-abstract bas-relief
on the gable end

The varying window sizes
hold a secret meaning

# MAISON DE LA CULTURE

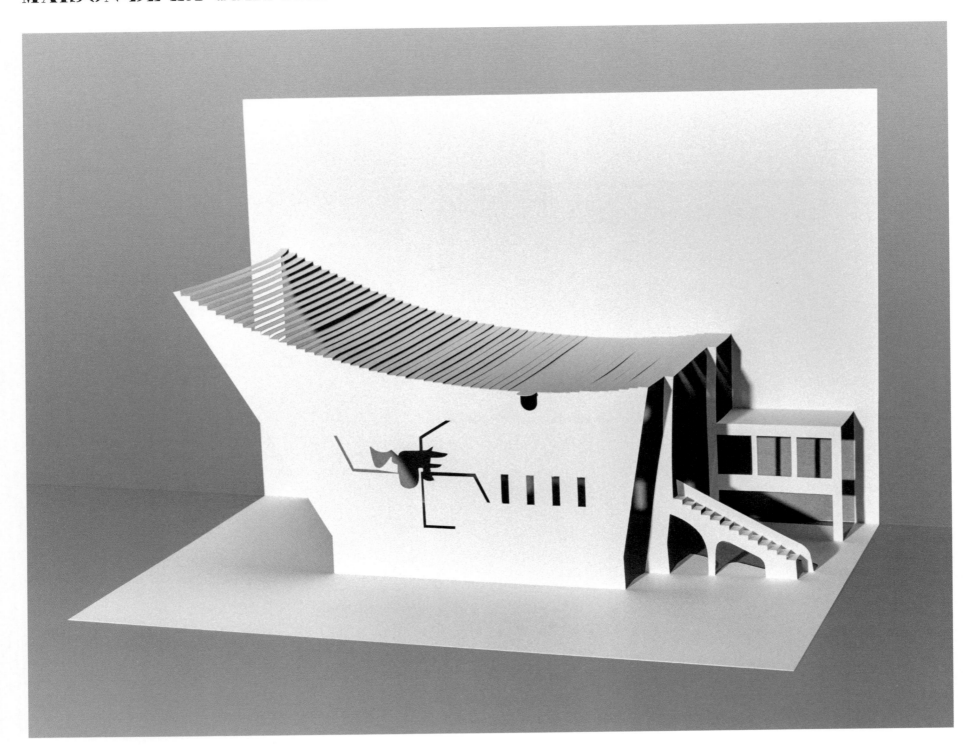

## Folding guide

**1** With the printed side facing you, lever fold the two horizon valley folds.

**2** Still with the printed side facing you, push out the valley folds at the base of the building.

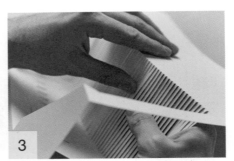

**3** Flipping between the front and the back of the model, push out and pinch the mountain folds and valley folds of the long strands that create the roof structure.

**4** Turn the template over to the blank side and crease the various mountain folds and valley folds of the side extension, including those of the staircase.

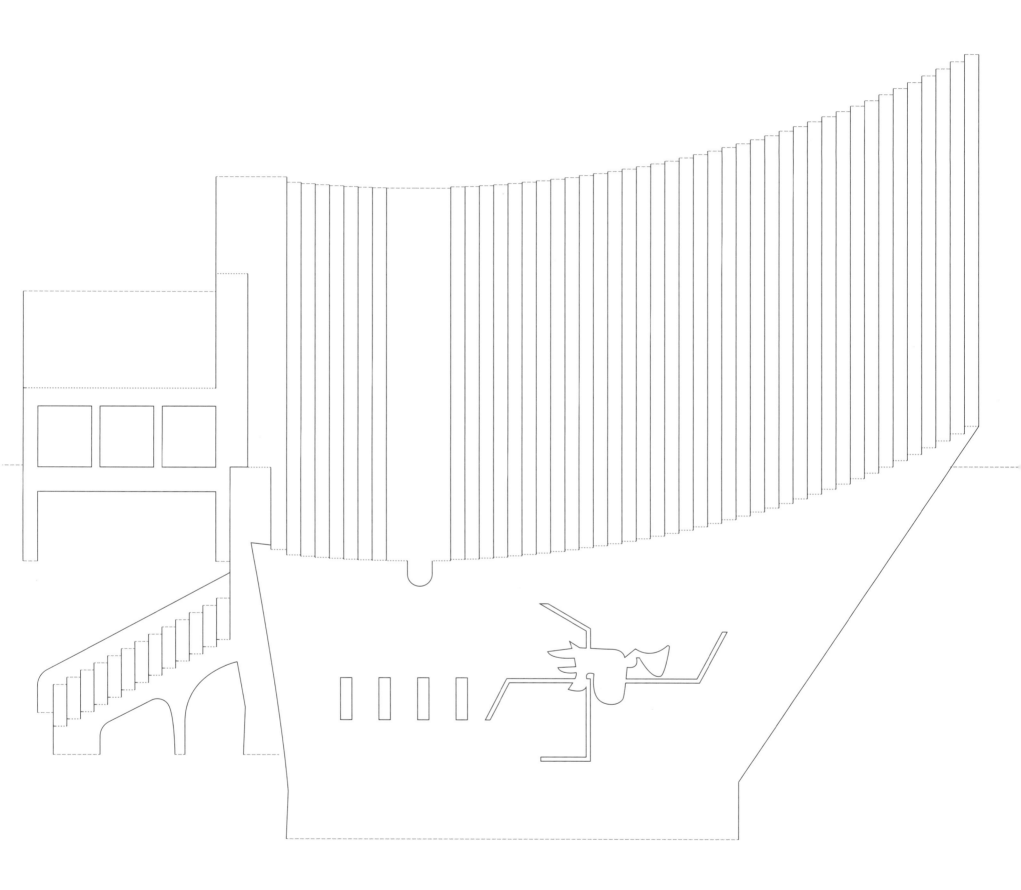

# VILLA SARABHAI

Ahmedabad, India, 1955

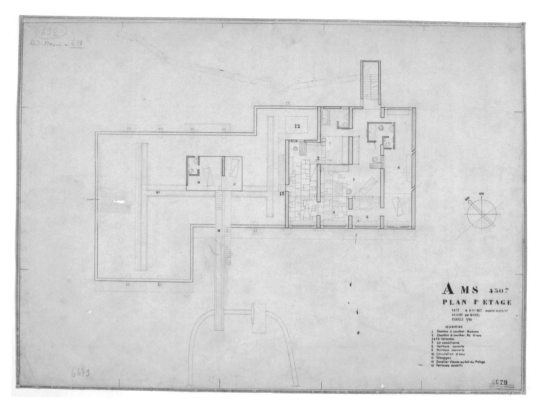

First-floor plan

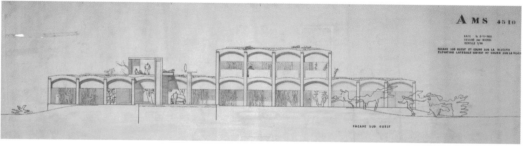

Garden elevation

The client, Madam Manorama, asked Le Corbusier to design a home for her and her two sons. Her brief requested a house without doors that would allow spaces to adapt to their needs – easily hosting her large extended family, or retracting into itself and creating private rooms.

It's clear that Villa Sarabhai shares the same 'genetic code' as Maisons Jaoul and Week-end. However, far removed from temperate France, Sarabhai would have to compete with the Indian climate by providing refuge from the tropical storms of monsoon seasons that could quickly alternate from torrential rain to sunshine.

Furthermore, unlike Maisons Jaoul, Sarabhai is low-profiled and nested deep into its grounds, a lush 8-hectare (20-acre) park. It is constructed of red brick with a roughcast concrete rendering, and is orientated to channel cooling north-easterly breezes.

Like Corbusier's previous buildings, Sarabhai's exterior reveals much of its internal structure. Load-bearing parallel walls create ten bays on the ground floor and four on the upper, both carrying a thick concrete roof and creating the main layout of long Catalan-vaulted rooms. Their cave-like interiors are protected from the scorching sunlight because each vault ends with a deep veranda overlooking the garden. These vault shapes aren't visible from the outside; instead, the house's elevations are accented with flat concrete caps. Water spouts dot the building, celebrating the fact that it must contend with monsoon downpours.

The soil and grass of the roof gardens help to cool the rooms below. And yes, your eyes don't deceive you – from the first-floor terrace, a concrete slide leads straight into the garden plunge pool. In contrast to the austere interior, I love this antithetical moment of glee.

There are no exterior doors; the verdant grounds flow into the interior. Bamboo curtains over the generous openings provide the only barrier to the outside, allowing air to circulate. Large pivoting walls between the parallel vaults mean that rooms can be combined to make larger spaces or divided for privacy.

A slide into the pool helps guests to cool off during the summer months

Vaulted spaces protect inhabitants from the sunlight

# VILLA SARABHAI

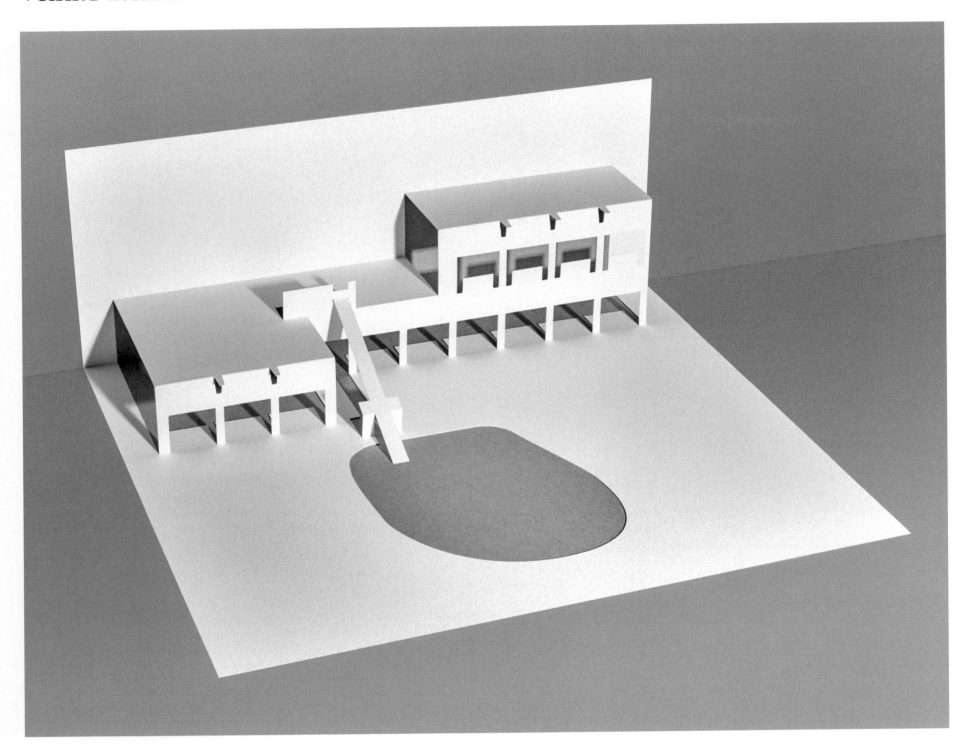

## Folding guide

**1** With the printed side facing you, start by lever folding the horizon valley folds, then push out all the valley folds that connect the roof of the building to the background plane.

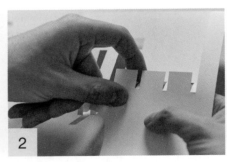

**2** Turn the template 180º and push out the valley-fold pillars at the base of the building.

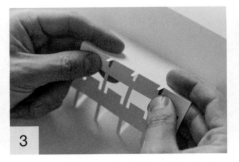

**3** Flip the model over to the blank side and pinch-crease the mountain folds along the rooflines of the building.

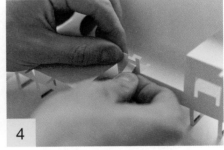

**4** Pull the tip of the slide towards you so that the fulcrum stands upright, and place the top end of the slide into the small slot to keep it in place.

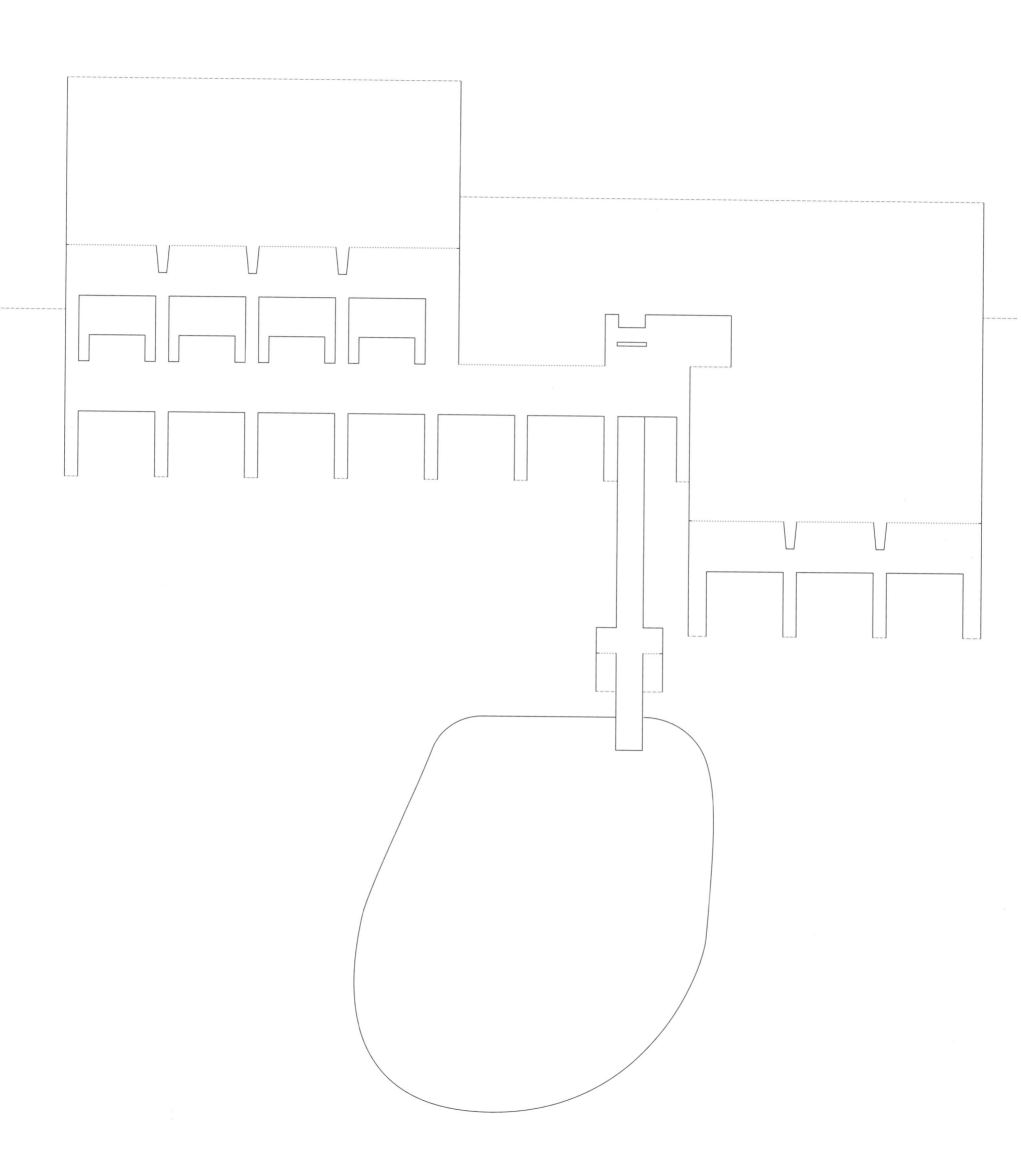

# HIGH COURT

Capitol, Chandigarh, India, 1955

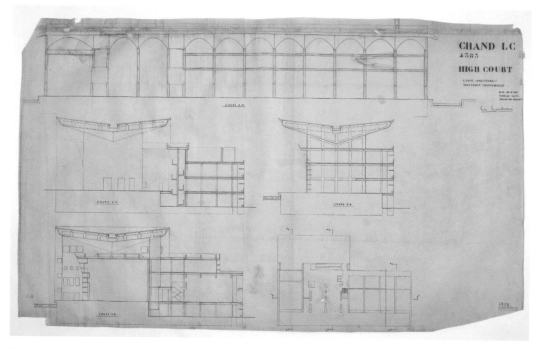

Section drawings

In 1950 Jawaharlal Nehru, the first Prime Minister of India, appointed Le Corbusier to plan the city of Chandigarh. Nehru envisaged it as '[u]nfettered by the traditions of the past, an expression of the nation's faith in the future'. Here, 260 kilometres (160 miles) north of New Delhi, the architect sought to create a model city of the future. It would be free from the nightmarish congestion that marred its neighbours, owing to his invention of the '7V' principle – a hierarchy of roads, from major highways (V1) to pedestrian walkways (V7). Laid down in a grid system, Chandigarh was originally divided into 52 interdependent sectors, each containing its own neighbourhoods, shops, medical buildings, places of worship and green space. There are now 56.

The High Court was the first part of the city's Capitol complex to be completed. In the Capitol's south-east corner, a monumental concrete canopy rests atop a wave of gently flowing arches. A trio of mammoth pillars, rising all the way from ground level to the top, splits the building into two separate blocks and forms an imposing floor-to-ceiling portico. Primary colours painted on the concrete rendering emphasize these pillars' scale. While the pillars and arches provide structural support to the canopy, it in turn affords protection to the building because it retreats under expansive brise-soleil. To the front of the High Court are enormous reflecting pools, bisected by road access to its portico.

People in Chandigarh are undoubtedly proud of their home, but the project faced criticism that Le Corbusier didn't sufficiently consider Indian culture in his design. Is forcing a society to act in a new way authentic? But despite this, Chandigarh remains a prosperous city – and many believe that, as it has surpassed its originally intended 500,000 inhabitants (the 2018 census records a population of 1.136 million), the theatrical bustle of a typical Indian city has woven itself back into the grid of this 'City of Tomorrow'.

In 2016 Chandigarh was recognized as a UNESCO World Heritage site.

The reflecting pools are often dry

Concrete pillar portico

# HIGH COURT

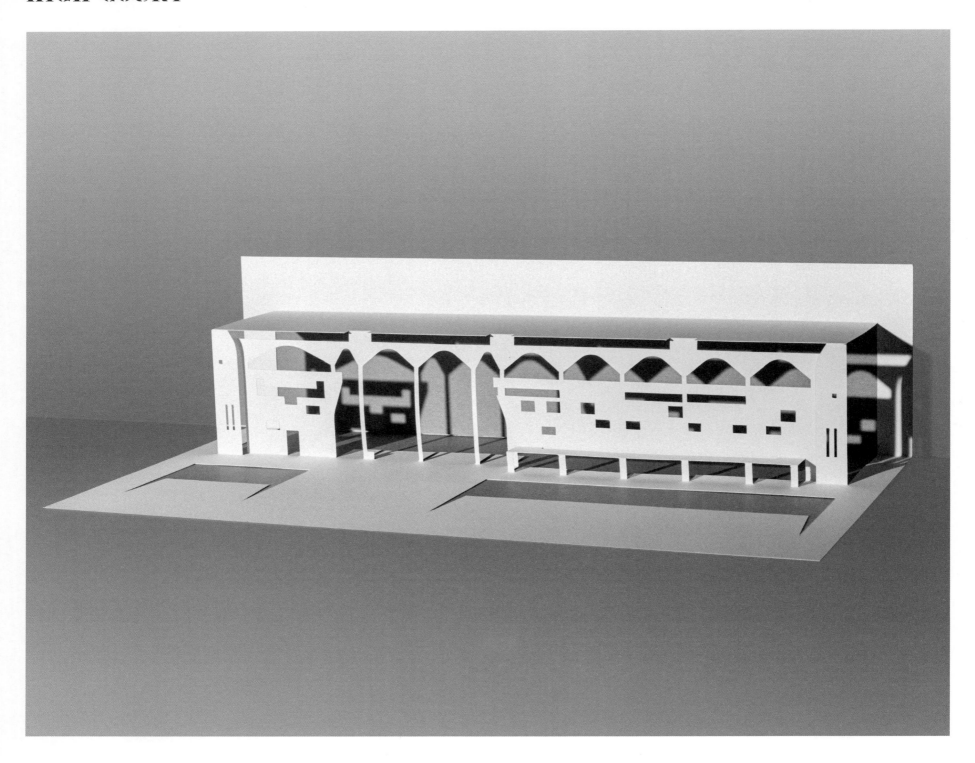

## Folding guide

**1** With the printed side facing you, lever fold the two horizon valley folds followed by the large valley fold that connects the top of the building to the background plane.

**2** Flip the model over and pinch your way across the five small mountain folds at the top and front of the building.

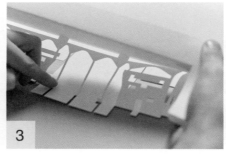

**3** Turn the model back over and push out all the valley folds at the base of the building, including those of the tall pillars.

**4** Form the veranda at the front of the building by flipping between the various folds at the front and back. It might help to use a skewer here, as the space is quite tight.

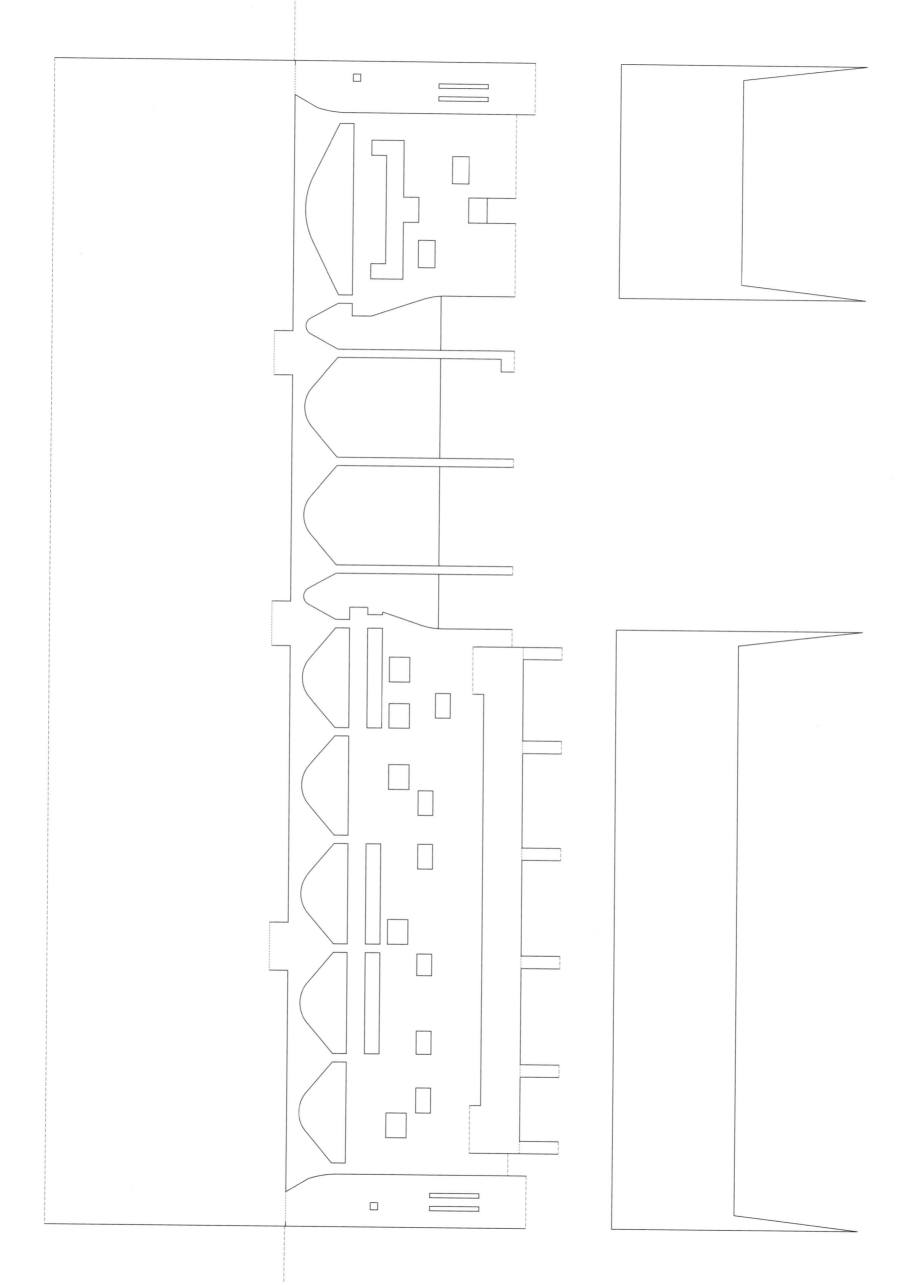

# CARPENTER CENTER FOR THE VISUAL ARTS

Cambridge, Massachusetts, USA, 1963

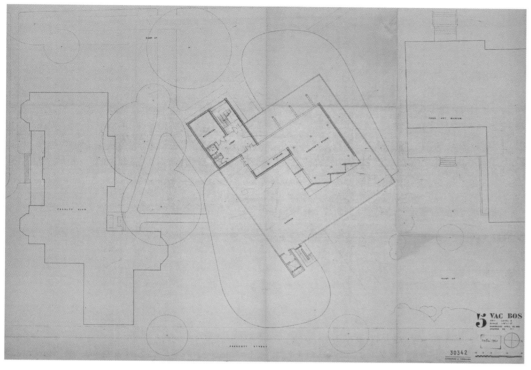

Floor plan; the curved studios
can be interpreted as lungs

In 1959 Le Corbusier was invited to construct a building for the arts department at Harvard University. Despite his long fascination with images of American industry, the architect – frustratingly – had not yet been given the opportunity to make his mark on US soil. The Carpenter Center would be his only work in North America.

The modest site sits between Quincy and Prescott streets. From the outset, Le Corbusier envisioned the building bridging the two thoroughfares. As you can imagine, the Center stands out among a sea of traditional red-brick neighbours – and not without controversy. Most notably, perhaps owing to his awareness that this might be his only chance to build in the US, the building carries characteristics of many of the architect's major themes – for example, the pilotis of his earlier Purist works, such as Villa Savoye, alongside the exposed concrete of Brutalism. It's notable that on this occasion, the architect insisted that the concrete exterior be polished and smooth to touch – apparently at great expense.

The Center has several distinctive features, and is formed of a variety of overlapping cubes and curves. Windows with angled baffles protect its interiors from direct sunlight. On opposite sides of the building, two large curved studios are raised on huge pillars, some as tall as 9 metres (30 feet). A tall core element houses the elevator.

Most interestingly, the building's heart is bisected by an S-shaped curving ramp snaking from one street side to the other. The site had previously been a park, and the design of the ramp allowed the public to pass through as they normally would have done. Once at the top of the ramp and within the heart of the building, the openness of the interior allowed the pedestrian a glimpse into the large studio spaces. An aerial view of the building can understandably be interpreted as a visual metaphor for the living machine – the two curved studios being seen as lungs, and its ramps as arteries.

A large curving ramp leads
up to the building

The large studio space

# CARPENTER CENTER FOR THE VISUAL ARTS

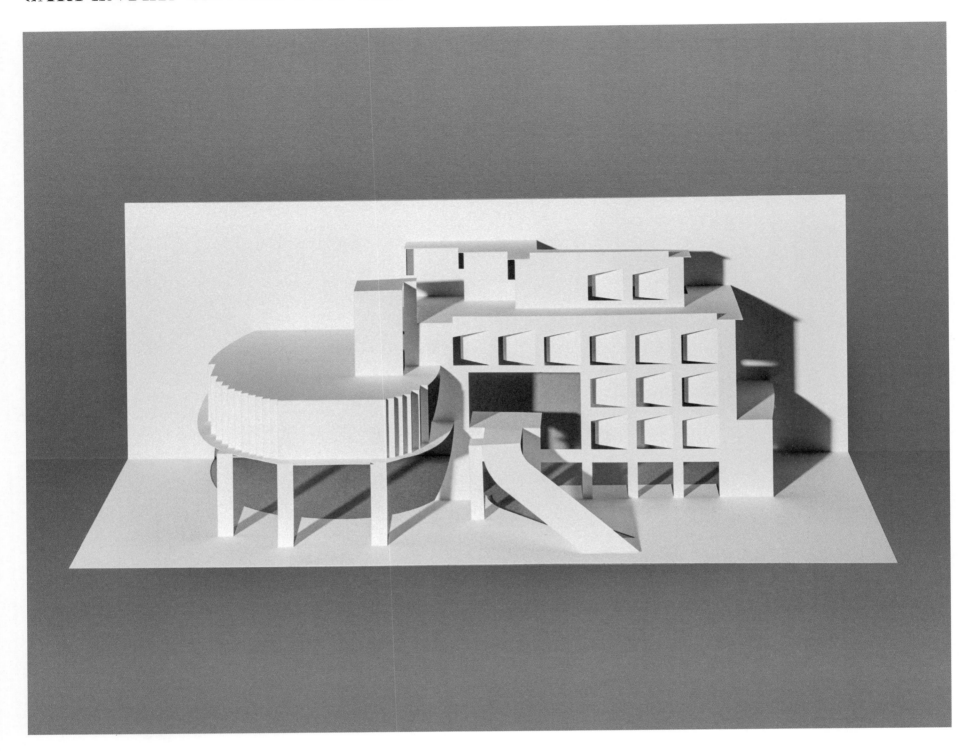

## Folding guide

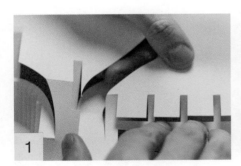

**1** With the printed side facing you, start by lever folding the horizon valley folds and then push out all the valley folds that connect the roof of the building to the background plane.

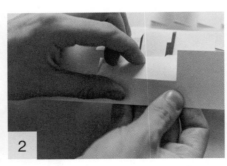

**2** Turn the template 180° and push out the valley-fold pillars at the base of the building.

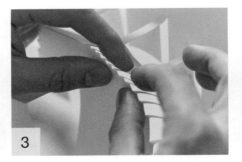

**3** Flip the model over to the blank side and pinch-crease the mountain folds along the rooflines of the building.

**4** Pull the tip of the slide towards you so that the fulcrum stands upright, and place the top end of the ramp into the small slot to keep it in place.

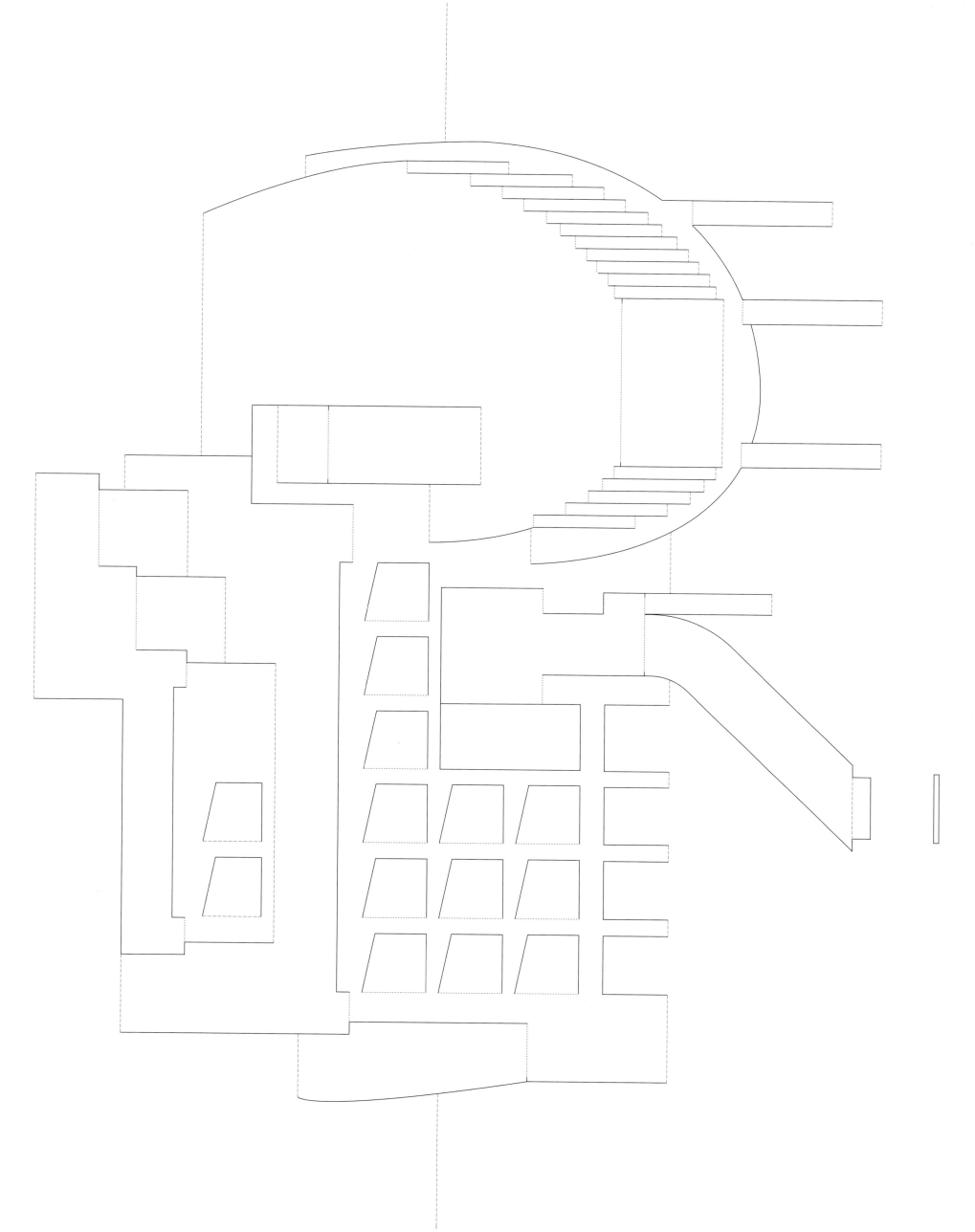